MW00513539

Ketogenic Slow Cooker Cookbook For Beginners

Simple, Easy and Irresistible Low Carb and Gluten Free Ketogenic Slow Cooker Recipes For Everyone

Sharon Scott

Disclaimer Notice:

Please note the information contained within this document is for educational and entertainment purposes only. All effort has been executed to present accurate, up to date, and reliable, complete information. No warranties of any kind are declared or implied. Readers acknowledge that the author is not engaging in the rendering of legal, financial, medical or professional advice. The content within this book has been derived from various sources. Please consult a licensed professional before attempting any techniques outlined in this book.

By reading this document, the reader agrees that under no circumstances is the author responsible for any losses, direct or indirect, which are incurred as a result of the use of information contained within this document, including, but not limited to, errors, omissions, or inaccuracies.

Table of Content

Introduction

Thank you for purchasing **Ketogenic Slow Cooker Cookbook For Beginners: Simple, Easy and Irresistible Low Carb and Gluten Free Ketogenic Slow Cooker Recipes For Everyone**

Cooking with a slow cooker, even though the times are obviously long, so much that it can take up to 10 hours for the most complex preparations, is very simple. Generally speaking, even the most modern models are limited to only two settings, that of time and temperature.

Usually the latter is chosen among three options, low, medium or high and in some cases there is also a "keep warm" button to keep food warm. Obviously the more we set the temperature high, the less time it will take to cook our food.

Speaking of costs, for a slow cooker you do not have to spend a fortune. On the market there are in fact even cheap and good brand around 50/60 dollars. We don't have to worry about spending on electricity, since despite the long cooking times, these products are designed not to consume large amounts of energy. The real big limitation is instead the size, which can make it difficult to place this product in smaller kitchens.

Breakfast Recipes

Breakfast Meatloaf

Preparation Time: 18 minutes

Cooking time: 7 hours

Servings: 8

Ingredients:

- 12 oz. ground beef

- 1 teaspoon salt

- 1 teaspoon ground coriander

- 1 tablespoon ground mustard

- ¼ teaspoon ground chili pepper

- 6 oz. white bread

- ½ cup milk

- 1 teaspoon ground black pepper

- 3 tablespoon tomato sauce

Directions:

1. Chop the white bread and combine it with the milk.

2. Stir then set aside for 3 minutes.

3. Meanwhile, combine the ground beef, salt, ground coriander, ground mustard, ground chili pepper, and ground black pepper.

4.   Stir the white bread mixture carefully and add it to the ground beef. Cover the bottom of the slow cooker bowl with foil.

5.   Shape the meatloaf and place the uncooked meatloaf in the slow cooker then spread it with the tomato sauce.

6.   Close the slow cooker lid and cook the meatloaf for 7 hours on LOW.

7.   Slice the prepared meatloaf and serve. Enjoy!

Nutrition: calories 214, fat 14, carbs 12, protein 9

Ham Pitta Pockets

Preparation Time: 14 minutes   Cooking time: 1.5 minutes

Servings: 6

Ingredients:

- 6 pita breads, sliced

- 7 oz. mozzarella, sliced

- 1 teaspoon minced garlic

- 7 oz. ham, sliced

- 1 big tomato, sliced

- 1 tablespoon mayo

- 1 tablespoon heavy cream

Directions:

1.   Preheat the slow cooker on HIGH for 30 minutes.

2.   Combine the mayo, heavy cream, and minced garlic.

3.   Spread the inside of the pita bread with the mayo mixture.

4.   After this, fill the pitta bread with the sliced mozzarella, tomato, and ham.Wrap the pita bread in foil and place them in the slow cooker.Close the slow cooker lid and cook the dish for 1.5 hours on HIGH.

5.   Then discard the foil and serve the prepared pita pockets immediately. Enjoy!

Nutrition: calories 273, fat 3, carbs 10, protein 10

Thyme Sausage Squash

Preparation Time: 15 minutes

Cooking time: 6 hours on low

Servings: 4

Ingredients:

- 2 tablespoons extra-virgin olive oil

- 14 ounces smoked chicken sausage, halved lengthwise and thinly sliced crosswise

- ¼ cup chicken broth

- 1 onion, halved and sliced

- ½ medium butternut squash, peeled, seeds and pulp removed, and diced

- 1 small green bell pepper, seeded and cut into 1-inch-wide strips

- ½ small red bell pepper, seeded and cut into 1-inch-wide strips

- ½ small yellow bell pepper, seeded and cut into 1-inch-wide strips

- ½ teaspoon freshly ground black pepper

- 1 cup shredded Swiss cheese

Directions:

1.   Combine all the ingredients. Cover and cook for 6 hours on low.

2.   Just before serving, sprinkle the Swiss cheese over the top, cover, and cook for about 3 minutes more to melt the cheese.

3.   Omit the cheese, and use a paleo-friendly sausage or diced ham.

Nutrition: calories 502, fat 26, carbs 13, protein 27

Onion Broccoli Quiche

Preparation Time: 10 minutes

Cooking time: 2 hours 30 minutes

Servings: 8

Ingredients:

- 9 eggs

- 2 cups cheese, shredded and divided

- 8 oz cream cheese

- 1/4 Tsp onion powder

- 3 cups broccoli, cut into florets

- 1/4 Tsp pepper

- 3/4 Tsp salt

Directions:

1.   Add broccoli into the boiling water and cook for 3 minutes. Drain well and set aside to cool.

2.   Add eggs, cream cheese, onion powder, pepper, and salt in mixing bowl and beat until well combined. Spray slow cooker from inside using cooking spray.

3.　　Add cooked broccoli into the slow cooker then sprinkle half cup cheese. Pour egg mixture over broccoli and cheese mixture.

4.　　Cover slow cooker and cook on high for 2 hours and 15 minutes.

5.　　Once it is done then sprinkle remaining cheese and cover for 10 minutes or until cheese melted. Serve warm and enjoy.

Nutrition: calories 296, fat 24, carbs 3, protein 16

Lunch recipes

Carrot Soup with Cardamom

Preparation time: 18 minutes

Cooking time: 12 hours

Servings: 9

Ingredients:

- 1-pound carrot
- 1 teaspoon ground cardamom
- ¼ teaspoon nutmeg
- 1 teaspoon salt
- 3 tablespoons fresh parsley
- 1 teaspoon honey
- 1 teaspoon marjoram
- 5 cups chicken stock
- ½ cup yellow onion, chopped
- 1 teaspoon butter

Directions:

1. Toss the butter in a pan and add chopped onion.

2. Chop the carrot and add it to the pan too.

3. Roast the vegetables for 5 minutes on the low heat.

After this, place the roasted vegetables in the slow cooker. Add ground cardamom, nutmeg, salt, marjoram, and chicken stock.

4. Close the slow cooker lid and cook the soup for 12 hours on LOW.

5. Chop the fresh parsley.

6. When the time is over, blend the soup with a hand blender until you get a smooth texture. Then ladle the soup into the serving bowls.

7. Sprinkle the prepared soup with the chopped fresh parsley and honey. Enjoy the soup immediately!

Nutrition:

Calories 80,

Fat 2.7,

Fiber 2,

Carbs 10.19,

Protein 4

Cod Chowder

Preparation time: 20 minutes

Cooking time: 3 hours

Servings: 6

Ingredients:

- 1 yellow onion

- 10 oz. cod

- 3 oz. bacon, sliced

- 1 teaspoon sage

- 5 oz. potatoes

- 1 carrot, grated

- 5 cups water

- 1 tablespoon almond milk

- 1 teaspoon ground coriander

- 1 teaspoon salt

Directions:

1. Peel the onion and chop it.

2. Put the chopped onion and grated carrot in the slow cooker bowl. Add the sage, almond milk, ground coriander, and water. After this, chop the cod into the 6 pieces.

3.   Add the fish in the slow cooker bowl too. Then chop the sliced bacon and peel the potatoes.

4.   Cut the potatoes into the cubes.

5.   Add the Ingredients: in the slow cooker bowl and close the slow cooker lid.

6.   Cook the chowder for 3 hours on HIGH. Ladle the prepared cod chowder in the serving bowls.

7.   Sprinkle the dish with the chopped parsley if desired. Enjoy!

Nutrition:

Calories 108,

Fat 4.5,

Fiber 2,

Carbs 8.02,

Protein 10

Hot Chorizo Salad

Preparation time: 20 minutes

Cooking time: 4 hours 30 minutes

Servings: 6

Ingredients:

- 8 oz. chorizo

- 1 teaspoon olive oil

- 1 teaspoon cayenne pepper

- 1 teaspoon chili flakes

- 1 teaspoon ground black pepper

- 1 teaspoon onion powder

- 2 garlic cloves

- 3 tomatoes

- 1 cup lettuce

- 1 cup fresh dill

- 1 teaspoon oregano

- 3 tablespoons crushed cashews

Directions:

1. Chop the chorizo sausages roughly and place them in the slow cooker.

2.   Cook the sausages for 4 hours on HIGH.

3.   Meanwhile, combine the cayenne pepper, chili flakes, ground black pepper, and onion powder together in a shallow bowl.

4.   Chop the tomatoes roughly and add them to the slow cooker after 4 hours. Cook the mixture for 30 minutes more on HIGH.

5.   Chop the fresh dill and combine it with oregano.

6.   When the chorizo sausage mixture is cooked, place it in a serving bowl. Tear the lettuce and add it in the bowl too.

7.   After this, peel the garlic cloves and slice them.

8.   Add the sliced garlic cloves in the salad bowl too.

9.   Then sprinkle the salad with the spice mixture, olive oil, fresh dill mixture, and crush cashew. Mix the salad carefully. Enjoy!

Nutrition:Calories 249, Fat 19.8,

Fiber 2,

Carbs 7.69,

Protein 11

Stuffed Eggplants

Preparation time: 20 minutes

Cooking time: 8 hours

Servings: 4

Ingredients:

- 4 medium eggplants
- 1 cup rice, half cooked
- ½ cup chicken stock
- 1 teaspoon salt
- 1 teaspoon paprika
- ½ cup fresh cilantro
- 3 tablespoons tomato sauce
- 1 teaspoon olive oil

Directions:

1. Wash the eggplants carefully and remove the flesh from them.

2. Then combine the rice with the salt, paprika, and tomato sauce.

3. Chop the fresh cilantro and add it to the rice mixture.

4. Then fill the prepared eggplants with the rice mixture.

5.   Pour the chicken stock and olive oil in the slow cooker.

6.   Add the stuffed eggplants and close the slow cooker lid.

7.   Cook the dish on LOW for 8 hours. When the eggplants are done, chill them little and serve immediately. Enjoy!

Nutrition:

Calories 277,

Fat 9.1,

Fiber 24,

Carbs 51.92,

Protein 11

Slow Cooker Risotto

Preparation time: 20 minutes

Cooking time: 3 hours 30 minutes

Servings: 6

Ingredients:

- 7 oz. Parmigiano-Reggiano

- 2 cup chicken broth

- 1 teaspoon olive oil

- 1 onion, chopped

- ½ cup green peas

- 1 garlic clove, peeled and sliced

- 2 cups long grain rice

- ¼ cup dry wine

- 1 teaspoon salt

- 1 teaspoon ground black pepper

- 1 carrot, chopped

- 1 cup beef broth

Directions:

1. Spray a skillet with olive oil.

2.   Add the chopped onion and carrot and roast the vegetables for 3 minutes on the medium heat. Then put the seared vegetables in the slow cooker. Toss the long grain rice in the remaining oil and sauté for 1 minute on the high heat.

3.   Add the roasted long grain rice and sliced garlic in the slow cooker.

4.   Add green peas, dry wine, salt, ground black pepper, and beef broth. After this, add the chicken broth and stir the mixture gently. Close the slow cooker lid and cook the risotto for 3 hours.

5.   Then stir the risotto gently.

6.   Shred Parmigiano-Reggiano and sprinkle over the risotto. Close the slow cooker lid and cook the dish for 30 minutes more. Enjoy the prepared risotto immediately!

Nutrition:

Calories 268,

Fat 3,

Fiber 4,

Carbs 53.34,

Protein 7

Dinner Recipes

Cube Steak

Preparation Time: 15 minutes Cooking Time: 8 hours

Servings: 8

Ingredients:

*   cubed steaks (28 oz.)

*   1 ¾ t. adobo seasoning/garlic salt

*   1 can (8 oz.) tomato sauce

*   1 c. water

*   Black pepper to taste

*   ½ med. onion

*   1 small red pepper

*   1/3 c. green pitted olives (+) 2 tbsp. brine

Directions:

Slice the peppers and onions into ¼-inch strips. Sprinkle the steaks with the pepper and garlic salt as needed and place them in the cooker.

Fold in the peppers and onion along with the water, sauce, and olives (with the liquid/brine from the jar). Close the lid.

Prepare using the low-temperature setting for eight hours.

Nutrition : Calories : 154 Net Carbs: 4 g Protein: 23.5 g Fat: 5.5 g

Ragu

Preparation Time: 10 minutes

Cooking Time: 8 hours

Servings: 2

Ingredients:

- ¼ of each - diced:

- 4 Carrot

- Rib of celery

- 1 Onion

- 1 minced garlic clove

- ½ lb. top-round lean beef

(3 oz.) of each:

- Diced tomatoes

- Crushed tomatoes

- 2 ½ t. beef broth (+) ¼ c.

1 ¼ t. of each:

- Chopped fresh thyme

- Minced fresh rosemary

- 1 bay leaf

- Pepper & Salt to taste

Directions:

Place the prepared celery, garlic, onion, and carrots into the slow cooker.

Trim away the fat and add the meat to the slow cooker.

Sprinkle with the salt and pepper

Stir in the rest of the ingredients.

Prepare on the low setting for six to eight hours. Enjoy any way you choose.

Nutrition:

Calories: 224

Net Carbs: 6 g

Protein: 27 g

Fat: 9 g

Main

Rabbit Stew

Preparation time: 15 minutes Cooking time: 5 hours

Servings: 6

Ingredients:

- 2 eggplants, chopped
- 1 zucchini, chopped
- 1 onion, chopped
- oz rabbit, chopped
- 2 cups water
- 1 tablespoon butter
- 1 teaspoon salt
- 1 teaspoon chili flakes

Directions:

Place the chopped eggplants, zucchini, onion, and rabbit in the slow cooker.

Add water, butter, salt, and chili flakes. Stir the stew gently and close the lid. Cook the stew for 5 hours on Low.

Then let the cooked rabbit stew cool slightly, then serve it!

Nutrition: calories 168, fat 6.1, fiber 7.2, carbs 13.6, protein 16.1

Garlic Sweet Potato

Preparation time: 10 minutes

Cooking time: 6 hours

Servings: 4

Ingredients:

- 2-pounds sweet potatoes, chopped

- 1 teaspoon minced garlic

- tablespoons vegan butter

- 1 teaspoon salt

- water

Directions

Pour water into the slow cooker. Add sweet potatoes.

Then add salt and close the lid.

Cook the sweet potato on Low for 6 hours.

After this, drain the water and transfer the vegetables in the big bowl.

Add minced garlic and butter. Carefully stir the sweet potatoes until butter is melted.

Nutrition 320 calories, 3.6g protein, 63.5g carbohydrates, 6.2g fat, 9.3g fiber, 15mg cholesterol, 648mg sodium, 1857mg potassium.

Stuffed Jalapenos

Preparation time: 10 minutes

Cooking time: 4.5 hours

Servings: 3

Ingredients:

*   jalapenos, deseed

*   oz. minced beef

*   1 teaspoon garlic powder

*   ½ cup of water

Directions

Mix the minced beef with garlic powder.

Then fill the jalapenos with minced meat and arrange it in the slow cooker.

Add water and cook the jalapenos on High for 4.5 hours.

Nutrition :

55 calories, 7.5g protein,

2.3g carbohydrates, 1.9g fat,

0.9g fiber, 0mg cholesterol,

2mg sodium,

71mg potassium.

Cilantro Meatballs

Preparation time: 20 minutes

Cooking time: 4 hours

Servings: 6

Ingredients:

- 1-pound minced beef

- 1 teaspoon minced garlic

- 1 egg, beaten

- 1 teaspoon chili flakes

- 2 teaspoons dried cilantro

- 1 tablespoon semolina

- ½ cup of water

- 1 tablespoon sesame oil

Directions

In the bowl, mix minced beef, garlic, egg, chili flakes, cilantro, and semolina.

Then make the meatballs.

After this, heat the sesame oil in the skillet.

Cook the meatballs in the hot oil on high heat for 1 minute per side.

Transfer the roasted meatballs to the slow cooker, add water, and close the lid.

Cook the meatballs on High for 4 hours.

Nutrition :

178 calories,

24.1g protein,

1.5g carbohydrates,

7.7g fat,

0.1g fiber,

95mg cholesterol,

61mg sodium,

321mg potassium.

Peppered Steak

Preparation time: 15 minutes Cooking time: 4 hours

Servings: 4 Ingredients:

- oz Sirloin Steak

- 2 cups water

- 1 tablespoon peppercorns

- ½ teaspoon ground nutmeg

- 2 garlic cloves, peeled

- 1 teaspoon olive oil

Directions:

Make the small cuts in the sirlion and chop the garlic cloves roughly.

Place the garlic cloves in the sirloin cuts.

Sprinkle the steak with the salt, ground nutmeg, and peppercorns.

Transfer the steak to the slow cooker and add water.

Close the lid and cook the steak for 4 hours on Low.

Then remove the steak from the slow cooker and slice it.

Enjoy!

Nutrition: calories 192, fat 12, fiber 4, carbs 1, protein 12

BBQ Beef Short Ribs

Preparation time: 10 minutes

Cooking time: 5 hours

Servings: 4

Ingredients:

- 1-pound beef short ribs

- ¼ cup of water

- 1/3 cup BBQ sauce

- 1 teaspoon chili powder

Directions

Rub the beef short ribs with chili powder and put in the slow cooker.

Mix water with BBQ sauce and pour the liquid into the slow cooker.

Cook the meat on High for 5 hours.

Nutrition :

266 calories, 32.8g protein,

7.9g carbohydrates, 10.4g fat,

0.3g fiber,

103mg cholesterol,

308mg sodium, 468mg potassium

Cilantro Beef

Preparation time: 10 minutes

Cooking time: 4.5 hours

Servings: 4

Ingredients:

- 1-pound beef loin, roughly chopped

- ¼ cup apple cider vinegar

- 1 tablespoon dried cilantro

- ½ teaspoon dried basil

- 1 cup of water

- 1 teaspoon tomato paste

Direction

Mix meat with tomato paste, dried cilantro, and basil.

Then transfer it to the slow cooker.

Cook the cilantro beef for 4.5 hours on High.

Nutrition 211 calories, 30.4g protein, 0.4g carbohydrates, 9.5g fat, 0.1g fiber, 81mg cholesterol, 66mg sodium, 412mg potassium.

Mashed Turnips

Preparation time: 10 minutes

Cooking time: 7 hours

Servings: 6

Ingredients:

* 3-pounds turnip, chopped

* 2 cup water

* 1 tablespoon vegan butter

* 1 tablespoon chives, chopped

* oz. Parmesan, grated

Directions

Put turnips in the slow cooker.

Add water and cook the vegetables on low for 7 hours.

Then drain water and mash the turnips.

Add chives, butter, and Parmesan.

Carefully stir the mixture until butter and Parmesan are melted. Then add chives. Mix the mashed turnips again.

Nutrition 162 calories, 8.6g protein, 15.1g carbohydrates, 8.1g fat, 4.1g fiber, 22mg cholesterol, 475mg sodium, 490mg potassium.

Soups, Stews, and Chilis

Slow Cooker Pierogie Casserole

Preparation Time: 15 minutes

Cooking time: 4 hours

Servings: 4

Ingredients:

- 3 tablespoons butter

- 1 head cabbage, chopped

- 1 onion, chopped

- 1-pound bacon

- 4 (16.9 ounce) packages of frozen pierogies

- 3 tablespoons butter

Directions:

1.   In a Dutch oven or a big pot, melt 3 tablespoons of butter over medium heat. Mix in onion and cabbage. Stir and cook for 20 minutes until the cabbage is soft.

2.   In a big, deep frying pan, put bacon and cook over medium-high heat for 10 minutes until turning brown evenly, flipping sometimes. Put the bacon slices on a dish lined with paper towels to strain. Slice the bacon into bite-sized pieces and put aside.

3.	Fully boil a big pot filled with lightly salted water over high heat. When the water boils, mix in pierogies and boil again. Cook for 5 minutes until the pierogies rise to the surface; strain.

4.	In a slow cooker, put the leftover 3 tablespoons of butter. Lightly mix bacon, cabbage, and pierogies; and put into the slow cooker. Cook for 3 hours on Low before eating.

Nutrition: calories 579, fat 18, carbs 33, protein 11

Hot and Sour Soup

Preparation Time: 15 minutes

Cooking time: 8 hours

Servings: 6

Ingredients:

* 1 package (10 oz.) packaged mushrooms, sliced

* 8 fresh shiitake mushroom caps, sliced

* 1 can (8 oz.) bamboo shoots, drained and julienned

* 4 garlic cloves, minced

* 1 package (15 oz.) tofu, cubed

* 2 tbsp. grated fresh ginger (divided)

* 4 cups water

* 2 tbsp. vegan chicken-flavored bouillon

* 2 tbsp. soy sauce

* 1 tsp. sesame oil

* 1 tsp. chili paste

* 2 tbsp. rice wine vinegar

* 1 1/2 cups peas, fresh or frozen

Directions:

1. Combine all the ingredients in the slow cooker.

2.   Cook for 6-8 hours on LOW. The mushrooms and bamboo shoots should be tender.

3.   Add the peas and remaining 1 tablespoon ginger. Stir.

4.   Adjust taste with vinegar or chili paste, if needed.

5.   Serve with a few more drops of sesame oil and the chili paste on the side. Enjoy!

Nutrition: calories 208, fat 7, carbs 22, protein 19

Peanut Soup (African Style)

Preparation Time: 17 minutes

Cooking time: 6 hours 10 minutes

Servings: 8

Ingredients:

- 1 yellow onion, diced

- 2 sprigs, chopped

- 2 red bell peppers, chopped

- 4 garlic cloves, minced

- 1 can (28 oz.) crushed tomatoes, undrained

- 8 cups vegetable broth

- 1/4 black pepper

- 1 tsp. ground cumin

- 1/4 tsp. chili powder

- 1/4 cup uncooked brown lentils

- 1/2 cup uncooked brown rice

- 1 cup peanut butter

- Sour cream and Tabasco sauce for topping

Directions:

1.   Combine the onions, peppers, garlic, tomatoes, broth, black pepper, cumin, chili powder, lentils, and rice in the slow cooker.

2.   Cover and cook for 6-8 hours on LOW or 4 hours on HIGH. The onions should be translucent.

3.   Stir in the butter and cook 30 minutes more on HIGH.

4.   Serve topped with sour cream and Tabasco sauce. Enjoy!

Nutrition: calories 245, fat 7, carbs 23, protein 10

Fish and Seafood

Cajun Shrimp

Preparation Time: 10 minutes Cooking time: 3 hours

Servings: 4

Ingredients:

- 1-pound shrimps, peeled

- 1 tomato, chopped

- 1 tablespoon keto tomato sauce

- 2 green bell peppers, chopped

- 1/3 teaspoon Cajun seasoning

- 1 teaspoon basil, dried

- 1 teaspoon oregano, dried

- 1 teaspoon salt

- ½ teaspoon ground black pepper

- ½ cup of water

Directions:

1.   Pour water into the slow cooker.

2.   Add shrimp and the other ingredients.

3.   Close the lid and cook liquid for 2 hours on High.

4.   Divide into bowls and serve.

Nutrition: calories 386, fat 2, carbs 5, protein 18

Tomato Shrimps

Preparation Time: 17 minutes

Cooking time: 10 minutes

Servings: 5

Ingredients:

- 8 oz king shrimps, peeled

- 1/4 cup keto tomato sauce

- 1 tablespoon sweet paprika

- 1 green chili pepper, chopped

- 2 tablespoons butter

- ¼ cup of water

- ½ teaspoon chili powder

Directions:

1. Pour water into the slow cooker.

2. Add the shrimp and the other ingredients, stir and close the lid.

3. Cook for 1 hour on High and serve.

Nutrition: calories 174, fat 12, carbs 3, protein 12

Balsamic Salmon

Preparation Time: 10 minutes

Cooking time: 1 hour

Servings: 3

Ingredients:

- 1-pound salmon fillet, sliced
- ½ teaspoon garlic powder
- ½ teaspoon salt
- ¼ teaspoon cayenne pepper
- 3 tablespoons balsamic vinegar
- 1/3 cup water
- ½ teaspoon olive oil

Directions:

1. In the slow cooker, mix the salmon with garlic powder, salt, and the other ingredients and toss gently.

2. Close the lid and cook salmon for 1 hour on High.

3. Serve the salmon with the balsamic sauce.

Nutrition: calories 226, fat 10, carbs 8, protein 20

Vegetables

Cauliflower Pilaf with Hazelnuts

Preparation time: 15 minutes

Cooking time: 2 hours

Servings: 6

Ingredients

- 3 cups cauliflower, chopped

- 1 cup chicken stock

- 1 teaspoon ground black pepper

- ½ teaspoon turmeric

- ½ teaspoon ground paprika

- 1 teaspoon salt

- 1 tablespoon dried dill

- 1 tablespoon butter

- 2 tablespoons hazelnuts, chopped

Directions:

1.   Put cauliflower in the blender and blend until you get cauliflower rice.

2.   Then transfer the cauliflower rice in the slow cooker.

3.   Add ground black pepper, turmeric, ground paprika, salt, dried dill, and butter.

4.   Mix up the cauliflower rice. Add chicken stock and close the lid.

5.   Cook the pilaf for 2 hours on High.

6.   Then add chopped hazelnuts and mix the pilaf well.

Nutrition: calories 48, fat 3.1, fiber 1.9, carbs 4.8, protein 1.6

VegetableCream

Preparation time: 15 minutes

Cooking time: 3 hours

Servings: 4

Ingredients

- 1 cup heavy cream

- 2 cups broccoli, chopped

- 2 spring onions, chopped

- 1 teaspoon olive oil

- 1 teaspoon salt

- 1 teaspoon ground paprika

- 1 oz. celery stalk, chopped

- 1 cup chicken stock

- 1 tablespoon fresh chives, chopped

- ½ cup mushrooms

Directions:

1. In the slow cooker, mix the broccoli with the onion and the other Ingredients, close the lid and cook on High for 3 hours.

2. Blend using an immersion blender and serve.

Nutrition: calories 218, fat 5.6, fiber 1.9, carbs 5.6, protein 4.4

Coconut Brussels Sprouts

Preparation time: 10 minutes

Cooking time: 4 hours

Servings: 6

Ingredients

- 2 cups Brussels sprouts, halved

- ½ cup of coconut milk

- 1 teaspoon garlic powder

- 1 teaspoon salt

- ½ teaspoon coriander, ground

- 1 teaspoon dried oregano

- 1 tablespoon balsamic vinegar

- 1 teaspoon butter

Directions:

1.   Place Brussels sprouts in the slow cooker.

2.   Add the rest of the Ingredients, toss, close the lid and cook the Brussels sprouts for 4 hours on Low.

3.   Divide between plates and serve.

Nutrition: calories 128, fat 5.6, fiber 1.7, carbs 4.4, protein 3.6

Coconut Okra

Preparation time: 15 minutes

Cooking time: 3 hours

Servings: 6

Ingredients

- 1-pound okra, trimmed

- 1/3 cup coconut cream

- 1/3 cup butter

- ½ teaspoon salt

- ½ teaspoon turmeric powder

- ¾ teaspoon ground nutmeg

Directions:

1.   In the slow cooker, mix the okra with cream, butter and the other Ingredients.

2.   Cook okra for 3 hours on High.

Nutrition: calories 203, fat 6.7, fiber 2.5, carbs 6.2, protein 3.3

Cauliflower Rice Mix

Preparation time: 15 minutes

Cooking time: 2 hours

Servings: 2

Ingredients

- 1 cup cauliflower rice

- 1 tablespoon coconut butter

- ¼ teaspoon salt

- ¾ teaspoon turmeric

- 1 teaspoon cayenne pepper

- 1 teaspoon curry powder

- 2 oz. Provolone cheese

- 1 ½ cups chicken stock

Directions:

1.   In the slow cooker, mix the cauliflower with the butter and the other Ingredients: except the cheese, close the lid and cook on High for 1 hour.

2.   Add the cheese, cook on High for 1 more hour, divide between plates and serve.

Nutrition: calories 131, fat 4.5, fiber 2.1, carbs 6.2, protein 4.5

Garlic Eggplant

Preparation time: 15 minutes

Cooking time: 2 hours

Servings: 4

Ingredients

- 1-pound eggplant, trimmed and roughly cubed
- 1 tablespoon balsamic vinegar
- 1 garlic clove, diced
- 1 teaspoon tarragon
- 1 teaspoon salt
- 1 tablespoon olive oil
- ½ teaspoon ground paprika
- ¼ cup of water

Directions:

1. In the slow cooker, mix the eggplant with the vinegar, garlic and the other Ingredients, close the lid and cook on High for 2 hours.

2. Divide into bowls and serve.

Nutrition: calories 132, fat 2.8, fiber 4.7, carbs 8.5, protein 1.6

Meat

BeefChops with Sprouts

Preparation time: 10 minutes Cooking time: 7 hours

Servings: 5

Ingredients

- 1-pound beef loin

- ½ cup bean sprouts

- 1 cup of water

- 1 tablespoon tomato paste

- 1 teaspoon chili powder

- 1 teaspoon salt

Directions

1   Cut the beef loin into 5 beef chops and sprinkle the beef chops with chili powder and salt. Then place them in the slow cooker. Add water and tomato paste. Cook the meat on low for 7 hours. Then transfer the cooked beef chops onto the plates, sprinkle with tomato gravy from the slow cooker, and top with bean sprouts.

Nutrition : 175 calories, 2 5.2g protein, 1.6g carbohydrates, 7.8g fat, 0.3g fiber, 64mg cholesterol, 526mg sodium, 386mg potassium.

Smoky Porkwith Cabbage

Preparation time: 10 minutes Cooking time: 8 hours

Servings: 6

Ingredients

- lbs. pastured pork roast
- 1/3 cup liquid smoke
- 1/2 cabbage head, chopped
- 1 cup water
- 1 tbsp. kosher salt

Directions:

1   Rub pork with kosher salt and place into the slow cooker. Pour liquid smoke over the pork. Add water.

2   Cover slow cooker with lid and cook on low for 7 hours.

3   Remove pork from the slow cooker and add cabbage to the bottom of the slow cooker.

4   Now place pork on top of the cabbage. Cover again and cook for 1 hour more. Shred pork with a fork and serves.

Nutrition: Calories 484 Fat 21.5 g Carbohydrates 3.5 g Sugar 1.9 g Protein 65.4 g Cholesterol 195 mg

Beef Ragout with Beans

Preparation time: 10 minutes

Cooking time: 5 hours

Servings: 5

Ingredients

- 1 tablespoon tomato paste

- 1 cup mug beans, canned

- 1 carrot, grated

- 1-pound beef stew meat, chopped

- 1 teaspoon ground black pepper

- 2 cups of water

Directions

1   Pour water into the slow cooker. Add meat, ground black pepper, and carrot.

2   Cook the mixture on High for 4 hours.

3   Then add tomato paste and mug beans. Stir the meal and cook it on high for 1 hour more.

Nutrition: 321 calories, 37.7g protein, 28g carbohydrates, 6.2g fat, 7.3g fiber, 81mg cholesterol, 81mg sodium, 959mg potassium.

Simple Roasted Pork Shoulder

Preparation time: 10 minutes

Cooking time: 9 hours

Servings: 8

Ingredients

*   lbs. pork shoulder

*   1 tsp garlic powder

*   1/2 cup water

*   1/2 tsp black pepper

*   1/2 tsp sea salt

Directions:

1   Season pork with garlic powder, pepper, and salt and place in a slow cooker. Add water.

2   Cover slow cooker with lid and cook on high for 1 hour, then turn heat to low and cook for 8 hours.

3   Remove meat from the slow cooker and shred using a fork.

4   Serve and enjoy.

Nutrition: Calories 664 Fat 48.5 g Carbohydrates 0.3 g Sugar 0.1 g Protein 52.9 g Cholesterol 204 mg

Pork Tenderloin

Preparation time: 10 minutes Cooking time: 4 hours

Servings: 6 Ingredients

- 1 ½ lbs. pork tenderloin, trimmed and cut in half lengthwise
- garlic cloves, chopped
- 1 oz enveloppe dry onion soup mix
- ¾ cup red wine
- 1 cup water
- Pepper and salt

Directions:

1   Place pork tenderloin into the slow cooker.

2   Pour red wine and water over pork. Sprinkle dry onion soup mix on top of pork tenderloin. Top with chopped garlic and season with pepper and salt. Cover slow cooker with lid and cook on low for 4 hours.

3   Stir well and serve.

Nutrition: Calories 196 Fat 4 g Carbohydrates 3.1 g Sugar 0.9 g Protein 29.9 g Cholesterol 83 mg

Hot Beef

Preparation time: 15 minutes

Cooking time: 8 hours

Servings: 4

Ingredients

- 1-pound beef sirloin, chopped

- 2 tablespoons hot sauce

- 1 tablespoon olive oil

- ½ cup of water

Directions

1   In the shallow bowl, mix hot sauce with olive oil.

2   Then mix beef sirloin with hot sauce mixture and leave
for 10 minutes to marinate.

3   Put the marinated beef in the slow cooker.

4   Add water and close the lid.

5   Cook the meal on Low for 8 hours.

Nutrition : 241 calories, 34.4g protein, 0.1g carbohydrates,
10.6g fat, 0g fiber, 101mg cholesterol, 266mg sodium, 467mg
potassium.

Side Dish Recipes

Okra and Corn

Preparation time: 15 minutes

Cooking time: 8 Hours

Servings: 4

Ingredients

- 3 garlic cloves, minced

- 1 small green bell pepper, chopped

- 1 small yellow onion, chopped

- 1 cup water

- 16 ounces okra, sliced

- 2 cups corn

- 1 and ½ teaspoon smoked paprika

- 28 ounces canned tomatoes, crushed

- 1 teaspoon oregano, dried

- 1 teaspoon thyme, dried

- 1 teaspoon marjoram, dried

- A pinch of cayenne pepper

- Salt and black pepper to the taste

Directions:

1. In your Crock Pot, mix garlic with bell pepper, onion, water, okra, corn, paprika, tomatoes, oregano, thyme, marjoram, cayenne, salt and pepper, cover, cook on Low for 8 hours, divide between plates and serve as a side dish.

Nutrition: calories 182, fat 3, fiber 6, carbs 8, protein 5

Savoy Cabbage Mix

Preparation time: 15 minutes

Cooking time: 2 Hours

Servings: 2

Ingredients

- 1 pound Savoy cabbage, shredded
- 1 red onion, sliced
- 1 tablespoon olive oil
- ½ cup veggie stock
- A pinch of salt and black pepper
- 1 carrot, grated
- ½ cup tomatoes, cubed
- ½ teaspoon sweet paprika
- ½ inch ginger, grated

Directions:

1.   In your Crock Pot, mix the cabbage with the onion, oil and the other Ingredients, toss, put the lid on and cook it on High for two hours.

2.   Divide the mix between plates and serve as a side dish.

Nutrition: calories 100, fat 3, fiber 4, carbs 5, protein 2

Blueberry Spinach Salad

Preparation time: 15 minutes

Cooking time: 1 Hour

Servings: 3

Ingredients

- ¼ cup pecans, chopped

- ½ tsp. sugar

- 2 tsp. maple syrup

- 1 tbsp. white vinegar

- 2 tbsp. orange juice

- 1 tbsp. olive oil

- 4 cups spinach

- 2 oranges, peeled and cut into segments

- 1 cup blueberries

Directions:

1.   Add pecans, maple syrup, and rest of the Ingredients: to the Crock Pot.

2.   Put the cooker's lid on and set the cooking time to 1 hour on High settings.

3.   Serve warm.

Nutrition: Per Serving: Calories: 140, Total Fat: 4g, Fiber: 3g, Total Carbs: 10g, Protein: 3g

Dill Mixed Fennel

Preparation time: 15 minutes

Cooking time: 3 Hour

Servings: 7

Ingredients

- 10 oz. fennel bulbs, diced

- 2 tbsp. olive oil

- 1 tsp. ground black pepper

- 1 tsp. paprika

- 1 tsp. cilantro

- 1 tsp. oregano

- 1 tsp. basil

- 3 tbsp. white wine

- 1 tsp. salt

- 2 garlic cloves

- 1 tsp. dried dill

Directions:

1. Add fennel bulbs and all other Ingredients: to the Crock Pot.

2.   Put the cooker's lid on and set the cooking time to 3.5 hours on High settings.

3.   Serve warm.

Nutrition: Per Serving: Calories: 53, Total Fat: 4.1g, Fiber: 2g, Total Carbs: 4g, Protein: 1g

Balsamic-glazed Beets

Preparation time: 15 minutes

Cooking time: 2 Hours

Servings: 6

Ingredients

- 1 lb. beets, sliced

- 5 oz. orange juice

- 3 oz. balsamic vinegar

- 3 tbsp. almonds

- 6 oz. goat cheese

- 1 tsp. minced garlic

- 1 tsp. olive oil

Directions:

1. Toss the beets with balsamic vinegar, orange juice, and olive oil in the insert of Crock Pot.

2. Put the slow cooker's lid on and set the cooking time to 7 hours on Low settings.

3. Toss goat cheese with minced garlic and almonds in a bowl.

4. Spread this cheese garlic mixture over the beets.

5.   Put the cooker's lid on and set the cooking time to 10 minutes on High settings.

6.   Serve warm.

Nutrition: Per Serving: Calories: 189, Total Fat: 11.3g, Fiber: 2g, Total Carbs: 12g, Protein: 10g

Jalapeno Meal

Preparation time: 15 minutes

Cooking time: 6 Hrs.

Servings: 6

Ingredients

- 12 oz. jalapeno pepper, cut in half and deseeded
- 2 tbsp. olive oil
- 1 tbsp. balsamic vinegar
- 1 onion, sliced
- 1 garlic clove, sliced
- 1 tsp. ground coriander
- 4 tbsp. water

Directions:

1. Place the jalapeno peppers in the Crock Pot.

2. Top the pepper with olive oil, balsamic vinegar, onion, garlic, coriander, and water.

3. Put the cooker's lid on and set the cooking time to 6 hours on Low settings.

4. Serve warm.

Nutrition: Per Serving: Calories: 67, Total Fat: 4.7g, Fiber: 2g, Total Carbs: 6.02g, Protein: 1g

Appetizers & Snacks

Garlic Parmesan Chicken Wings

Preparation time: 10 Minutes

Cooking time: 3 Hours 20 Minutes

Servings: 8

Ingredients

- 1 cup Parmesan Cheese, shredded

- lb. Chicken Wings

- ¼ tsp. Black Pepper, grounded

- ½ cup Butter, preferably organic

- 1 tsp. Sea Salt

- Garlic cloves, finely minced

Directions:

1   Begin by placing the chicken wings in the bottom portion of the slow cooker. After that, butter a large skillet over medium heat, and to this, add the garlic.

2   Sauté the garlic for 30 to 50 seconds or until aromatic. Spoon in the oil over the chicken wings and coat them well.

3   Now, cook them for 3 hours on low heat. Toward the end time, preheat the oven to broil.

4   Line the baking sheet using a parchment paper. Once the chicken is cooked, transfer them to the baking sheet in a single layer.

5   Broil it within 5 minutes or until the chicken is golden brown in color and crispy. Bring the baking sheet out after 5 minutes and top it with the cheese.

6   Return the sheet to oven and bake for another 2 minutes or until melted.

Nutrition:

Calories: 426

Fat: 34g

Carbohydrates: 1g

Proteins: 27g

Cocoa Nuts

Preparation time: 5 Minutes

Cooking time: 1 Hour

Servings: 6

Ingredients

- ½ cup Walnuts

- tbsp. Swerve

- ½ cup Almonds, slivered

- tbsp. Butter softened

- ½ cup Pecans, halved

- 2 tbsp. Cocoa Powder, unsweetened

- 1 tsp. Vanilla Extract

Directions:

1   First, place all the Ingredients needed to make this snack in a large mixing bowl. Mix well until well combined.

2   Transfer the nut mixture to the slow cooker—Cook within 1 hour on high heat.

3   Once the cooking time is up, place them on a baking sheet and cool before storing.

Nutrition:

Calories: 218

Fat: 21g

Carbohydrates: 2g

Proteins: 4g

Tex-Mex CheeseDip

Preparation time: 15 minutes

Cooking time: 1 hour & 30 minutes

Servings: 6

Ingredients

- ounces Velveeta cheese, cubed

- ¾ cup diced tomatoes with green chili peppers

- 1 teaspoon taco seasoning

Directions:

1   In a slow cooker, place Velveeta cheese cubes.

2   Cook on low and cook, covered, for about 30-60 minutes, stirring occasionally.

3   Uncover the slow cooker and stir in tomatoes and taco seasoning. Cook, covered, for about 30 minutes Serve hot.

Nutrition:Calories: 114 Carbohydrates: 5.2gProtein: 7g Fat: 8.1gSugar: 3.4g Sodium: 577mgFiber: 0.3g

2-Ingredient Cheese Dip

Preparation time: 15 minutes

Cooking time: 2 hours

Servings: 20

Ingredients

- 16 ounces Velveeta cheese, cubed

- 1 (16-ounce) jar salsa

Directions:

1 In a large slow cooker, place cheese and salsa and stir gently to combine.

2 Cook on high, covered, for about 2 hours, stirring occasionally. Serve hot.

Nutrition:

Calories: 71

Carbohydrates: 3.9gProtein: 4.4g

Fat: 4.9gSugar: 2.3g

Sodium: 460mg

Fiber: 0.4g

Candied Pecans

Preparation time: 5 Minutes

Cooking time: 3 Hours

Servings: 12

Ingredients

- 1 cup Sukrin Gold

- 1 Egg White, medium-sized

- cups Pecan

- ¼ cup Water

- tsp. Vanilla Extract

- 1 ½ tbsp. Cinnamon

Directions:

1   First, butter the insides of the slow cooker and transfer the pecans to it.

2   After that, mix vanilla extract and egg white in a mixing bowl until just combined and foamy.

3   Spoon this egg mixture over the pan. Stir them so that they coat the pecans well. Now, combine the cinnamon with the Sukrin Gold until well incorporated.

4   Pour the batter over the pecans and stir them again.

5   Then, close the lid and cook for 3 hours on low heat while stirring them every quarter of an hour.

6   Once the time is up, transfer the pecans to a baking sheet in a single layer and allow it to cool. Serve and enjoy.

Nutrition:

Calories: 257

Fat: 26g

Carbohydrates: 4g

Proteins: 4g

Swiss Style Cheese Fondue

Preparation time: 15 minutes

Cooking time: 3 hours & 10 minutes

Servings: 6

Ingredients

- 1 clove garlic, cut in half
- 2½ cups homemade chicken broth
- tablespoons fresh lemon juice
- 16 ounces Swiss cheese, shredded
- ounces Cheddar cheese, shredded
- tablespoons almond flour
- Pinch of ground nutmeg
- Pinch of paprika
- Pinch of ground black pepper

Directions:

1   Rub a pan evenly with cut garlic halves. Add broth and place pan over medium heat.

2   Cook until mixture is just beginning to bubble. Adjust to low, then stir in lemon juice.

3   Meanwhile, in a bowl, mix cheeses and flour. Slowly, add cheese mixture to broth, stirring continuously.

4   Cook until cheese mixture becomes thick, stirring continuously. Transfer the cheese mixture to a greased slow cooker and sprinkle with nutmeg, paprika, and black pepper.

5   Cook in the slow cooker on low, covered, for about 1-3 hours.

Nutrition:

Calories: 479 Carbohydrates: 6.1g

Protein: 32.6g

Fat: 36g

Sugar: 1.8g

Sodium: 700mg

Fiber: 0.5g

Desserts

Vanilla Chocolate Walnut Fudge

Preparation Time: 10 minutes

Cooking time: 2 hours

Servings: 12

Ingredients:

- Coconut oil, for coating the slow cooker insert and a baking dish
- 1 cup canned coconut milk
- 4 ounces unsweetened chocolate, chopped
- 1 cup erythritol
- 2 teaspoons stevia powder
- ¼ teaspoon fine sea salt
- 2 teaspoons pure vanilla extract
- 1 cup chopped toasted walnuts

Directions:

1. Generously coat the inside of the slow cooker insert with coconut oil.

2. In a large bowl, whisk the coconut milk into a uniform consistency. Add the chocolate, erythritol, stevia powder, and

sea salt. Stir to mix well. Pour into the slow cooker. Cover and cook for 2 hours on low.

3.   When finished, stir in the vanilla.

4.   Let the fudge sit in the slow cooker, with the lid off, until it cools to room temperature, about 3 hours.

5.   Coat a large baking dish with coconut oil and set aside.

6.   Stir the fudge until it becomes glossy, about 10 minutes.

7.   Stir in the walnuts. Transfer the mixture to the prepared baking dish and smooth it into an even layer with a rubber spatula. Refrigerate overnight. Serve chilled, cut into small pieces.

Nutrition: calories 126, fat 6, carbs 3, protein 7

Shredded Coconut-Raspberry Cake

Preparation Time: 10 minutes

Cooking time: 3 hours

Servings: 10

Ingredients:

- ½ cup melted coconut oil, plus more for coating the slow cooker insert
- 2 cups almond flour
- 1 cup unsweetened shredded coconut
- 1 cup erythritol or 1 teaspoon stevia powder
- ¼ cup unsweetened, unflavored protein powder
- 2 teaspoons baking soda
- ¼ teaspoon fine sea salt
- 4 large eggs, lightly beaten
- ¾ cup canned coconut milk
- 1 teaspoon coconut extract
- 1 cup raspberries, fresh or frozen

Directions:

1. Generously coat the inside of the slow cooker insert with coconut oil.

2.	In a large bowl, stir together the almond flour, coconut, erythritol, protein powder, baking soda, and sea salt.

3.	Whisk in the eggs, coconut milk, ½ cup of coconut oil, and coconut extract.

4.	Gently fold in the raspberries.

5.	Transfer the batter to the prepared slow cooker, cover, and cook for 3 hours on low. Turn off the slow cooker and let the cake cool for several hours, to room temperature. Serve at room temperature.

Nutrition: calories 406, fat 8, carbs 13, protein 19

CPSIA information can be obtained
at www.ICGtesting.com
Printed in the USA
BVHW051328280321
603262BV00046B/703